SKILL OF LISTENING   EARLY INTERMEDIATE

Loud and Clear

Rosemary Aitken

Nelson

Thomas Nelson and Sons Ltd
Nelson House Mayfield Road
Walton-on-Thames Surrey KT12 5PL

51 York Place
Edinburgh EH1 3JD

Thomas Nelson (Hong Kong) Ltd
Toppan Building 10/F
22A Westlands Road
Quarry Bay Hong Kong

Distributed in Australia by

Thomas Nelson Australia
480 La Trobe Street
Melbourne Victoria 3000
and in Sydney, Brisbane, Adelaide and Perth

© Rosemary Aitken 1983

First published by Thomas Nelson and Sons Ltd 1983
Reprinted 1984, 1985, 1986

ISBN 0-17-555-460-9

NCN 73-ESK-9006-04

All Rights Reserved. This publication is protected in the United Kingdom by the Copyright Act 1956 and in other countries by comparable legislation. No part of it may be reproduced or recorded by any means without the permission of the publisher. This prohibition extends (with certain very limited exceptions) to photocopying and similar processes, and written permission to make a copy or copies must therefore be obtained from the publisher in advance. It is advisable to consult the publisher if there is any doubt regarding the legality of any proposed copying.

Printed in Hong Kong

Acknowledgements

Illustrations
pp. 9, 13, 21, 30, 36, 41 and 45 Dave Harris
pp. 10, 15, 18, 22, 26, 34 and 46 Nigel Paige
p. 47 Julia Whatley

Contents

1 I am Michael Roberts' granddaughter — *page 4*

2 Birthday Surprise! — *page 8*

3 Which one is Chepstow Castle? — *page 12*

4 Come out! We know you're there! — *page 16*

5 We can use the school hall — *page 20*

6 Miles from anywhere — *page 24*

7 The monster will come back! — *page 28*

8 There must be some mistake — *page 32*

9 The ugliest jug you've ever seen! — *page 36*

10 Amazing Journey — *page 40*

11 Consolidation: Anyone for cricket? — *page 44*

UNIT ONE
I am Michael Roberts' granddaughter

1 Read and listen
Last month this paragraph was in a London newspaper:

Camden Guardian 6 June 1980

Lucky Lady inherits £500,000

Michael Roberts, a London taxi driver for many years, died last month at his home in Camden. He was ninety-three. Police found no food in the house, and very little furniture. But there was £500,000 in a box under the bed. In his will, Mr. Roberts left everything to his granddaughter, Judith. She was born in London in 1941, and now lives somewhere in India. Police do not know her address, but policemen in Delhi are looking for the lucky lady, who will inherit £500,000 and her grandfather's house.

Yesterday a young woman arrived at a police station in South London. 'I am Michael Roberts' granddaughter,' she said. Listen to her story. Is she telling the truth?

2 Find the mistakes
While the young lady was talking, a policeman made notes about what she said. Here are some things he made notes about. Can you find any mistakes in the young lady's story?

a) Age
b) Life in India
c) Letter to her grandfather
d) Letters from her grandfather
e) Parents
f) Anything suspicious

3 Talk to the press

When she left the police station, the young woman talked to a journalist. Write the interview. Use these words to help you.

—Who____?
—When____?
—Where____?
—How____?
—Why____?
—What____?
—How much____?

4 Describe Judith

Here is a photo of the real Judith. The police found it in her grandfather's house. Write a description for the Delhi police. Tell them about:

—Height (Short / medium height / tall / very tall)
—Build (Thin / slim / plump / fat)
—Colour of hair (Fair / dark / grey-haired)
—Age (Young / middle-aged / old / elderly)
—Any other distinguishing marks.

(Remember that people do not always wear the same clothes.)

5 Find the message

The police did not find Judith. She came to them. The day before he died Michael Roberts wrote her a letter. He was very ill and his writing was very bad so at first she did not understand it. Can you help her?

> Mydearjudithcomehomeatoncethereis halfamillionpoundsinaboxundermybed andiamleavingitalltoyouyoumustgotothe policeandshowthemthisletterbecausemany otherpeoplewillclaimthemoneyishalltellthe policeinlondonthatiamwritingtoyousocome homequicklyandgostraighttothemyourloving grandfathermichaelroberts.

6 What did she say?

When people heard about Judith, a radio reporter tried to telephone her in India. Unfortunately the line was very bad, and he couldn't hear everything that she said. What did she say?

Reporter: Well Judith, how did you feel when you heard about your grandfather's will?
Judith: I was ____lighted about the money, ____ course, but I was upset when I ____ about my grandfather's death. ____ loved him very ____.
Reporter: Did you know him well?
Judith: No, I only met ____ once when I came ____ England with my mother. I was eight years ____. But I remember him. He was very ____ to me, and when I came ____ to India he wrote a letter ____ me every week.
Reporter: Well, congratulations, Judith.
Judith: ____ you very much.

7 Work it out

When the police first came to Michael Roberts' house, they found a message in code. Here is the code. Work out what the numbers mean and find out what the message says.

13-25   13-15-14-5-25   9-19   9-14   1   2-15-24
21-14-4-5-18   20-8-5   2-5-4   20-8-5   11-5-25   9-19
15-14   20-8-5   2-15-15-11-3-1-19-5

A B C D E F G H I J K L M N O
1   5   8

P Q R S T U V W X Y Z

UNIT TWO
Birthday Surprise!

1 Listen
It's Jim's birthday today. He is staying with his grandparents on their farm, and when he woke up this morning he hoped to find his birthday present in his bedroom. He found a little parcel on the table, and he untied the string. Inside the parcel there was a cassette. He played it on his portable cassette recorder.

Look at the map and listen to what he heard.

2 Listen and follow
Look at the map. Can you help Jim find his birthday present? Do you know what it is?

3 Give directions
Can you help Jim get from the front door to his 'present' a quicker way? Give him directions.

4 Which animals escaped?
One of Jim's friends came to look at his present. He arrived at the bus stop and he walked up the path, through the pigs' field, and the empty field to the yard. Unfortunately he forgot to close the gates. Jim's grandmother was very upset. Here are some of the things she said:

a) The bull will escape.
b) The cows will get on to the road.
c) The horses will get out.
d) The pigs will get into the orchard.
e) The lambs will get into the field with the cows.
f) The pigs will get into the field with the sheep.
g) The orchard will be full of cows.
h) The pigs will come into the yard.

Fortunately, not all of these things happened. Some of them were not possible because the boy only opened the gates on his way. Work out which of Jim's grandmother's worries were unnecessary.

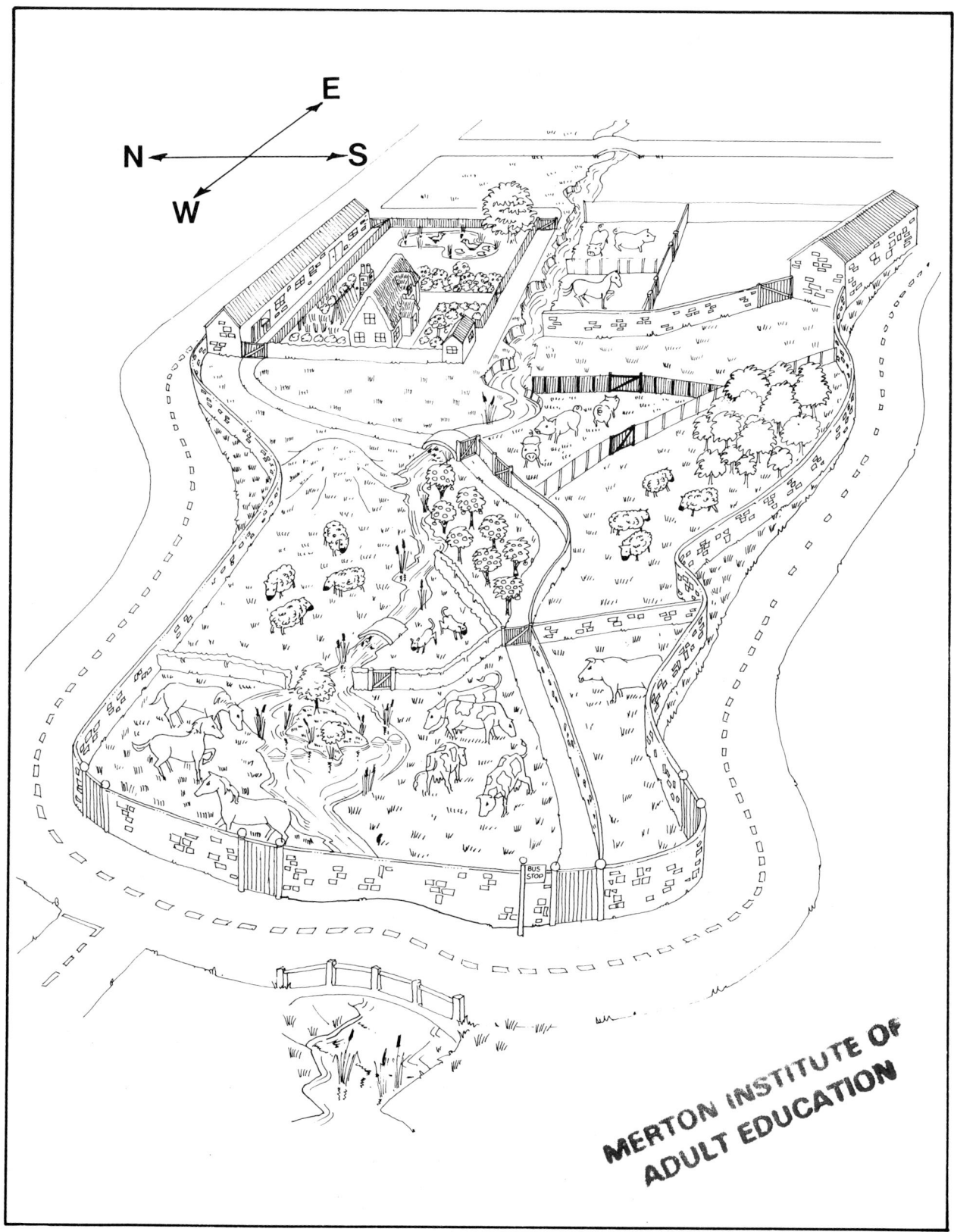

5 Find the way

They found some animals in the wrong places:
–Some pigs were on the road.
–One pig was in the orchard.
–Three cows were in the yard.
–One cow was in the empty field.
How did they get there?

Jim's friend hid on the island. How did he get there?

6 Sort it out

Jim's friend loved the farm. When he went home he told his mother all about it. But he was so excited he mixed up all the sentences. Can you sort them out?

a) I left the gates   on the stepping-stones.
b) I had lunch   in the river.
c) The pigs are   very excited.
d) Jim is   open.
e) There are two bridges   in the farmhouse.
f) You can walk   over the water.
g) The stepping-stones are   white and woolly.
h) The lambs are   pink and fat.

7 Find the name

Write down the names of these seven things. The first letter of each thing will spell the name of Jim's friend.

a) We get milk from this animal. ____
b) Jim's birthday present was a ____.
c) Pigs, sheep and cows are all ____ that live on a farm.
d) All the bridges on the farm go over the same ____.
e) Baby sheep are called ____.
f) A big grey animal with a long nose that lives in a zoo, and comes from Africa or India. ____
g) We get wool from these animals. ____

What is the name of Jim's friend?

UNIT THREE
Which one is Chepstow Castle?

1 Read and listen

Mr Wilkins is an excellent artist. One day he receives this note from his son, Brian, who is a university student.

Dear Dad,

I called to see you but you weren't in. Have you still got those sketches which you drew in Wales? I met a very nice girl at a party last night, and I'm going to meet her again tonight. She's going to Wales for her holiday, and she says she is especially interested in Chepstow Castle. I know you drew several pictures of it when you were there. Can you bring one or two sketches to my flat this afternoon please? When I am with a girl I never know what to say, but if we have your sketches we can talk about those.

Thanks.
Brian

Later in the day Brian telephones his father. Listen to part of their conversation.

2 Find the castle
Look at the three drawings. Which one is Chepstow Castle?

3 Describe the castles

Brian showed Janet the sketches of the castles and she asked him some questions. But he was very shy and he did not say very much.
She said, 'What is the castle like?', and he said, 'Big'.
She said, 'What is the river like?', and he said, 'Deep'.

Here are some more questions which Janet asked. What do you think Brian said?

–What are the trees like?
–What is the gate like?
–What are the towers like?
–What is the rockface like?
–What is the scenery like?
–What are the walls like?
–What are the windows like?
–What was the weather like?
–What was the holiday like?

4 Compare the castles

Janet looked at the sketches. 'These are excellent drawings', she said. 'Do you know anything about castles?'
'Not much', said Brian.

Look at the pictures. Which castle do you think is the oldest?

Brian said, 'Castle A looks older than Castle B, but I think Castle C is the oldest of all'.
Janet said, –'Which castle do you think was the strongest?'
              –'Which do you think was the most comfortable?'
              –'Which do you think is the biggest?'
              –'Which do you think is the most beautiful?'
              –'Which do you think is the most interesting?'
              –'Which do you think is the best drawing?'

What do you think? Give a reason for your choices.

5 Consider the colours

Brian's father is going to paint a larger picture of Kilchurn Castle (Sketch B). He made some notes about the colours he wants to use. What do you think he is going to use these colours for?

dark grey
deep blue
dim purple
misty green
light brown
pale blue
bright red
vivid gold

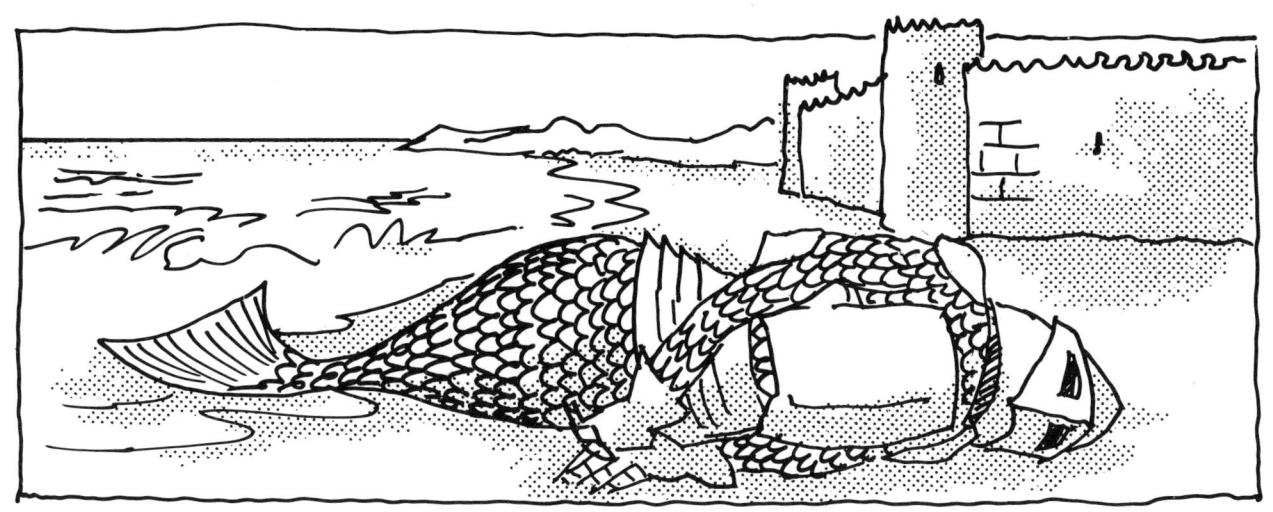

6 Who said what?

In the restaurant Brian and Janet both started to talk at once. Brian talked about fishing and Janet talked about soldiers. This is what a man at the next table heard. Who said what?

I can imagine the soldiers.   There are hundreds of them in the river.   Some of them are three feet long.   They used to carry torches.   They used to walk on top of the walls.   They have long tails.   They swim very fast.   They used to throw things from the walls at their enemies.   If you pull one into a boat it will try to bite you.   They like to eat insects.   They live in mud at the bottom of the river.   Some of them used to ride horses.   I wonder what they used to wear.   I like to fry them with butter and eat them straight away.   They used to be very brave.   Would you like to catch one?

7 Work it out

The story of Janet and Brian does not end there. Here is part of Janet's diary. She wrote it in code because she did not want her sister to read it. This is a list of the places where Janet and Brian went. All the letters are mixed up. Can you work out what it says? Start with the capital letter. The first one is done to help you.

a) 21 June   tauRnestar   Restaurant
b) 22 June   neCmia
c) 29 June   leaCst
d) 6 July   oncreCt
e) 13 July   rateeTh
f) 20 July   scioD
g) 27 July   caneD
h) 3 August   trayP
i) 2 January   dingdeW

UNIT FOUR
Come out! We know you're there!

1 Read and listen
Keith Adams is writing a letter to his grandparents.

> 23 Middlefield Road
> London
>
> 25 September
>
> Dear Gran and Grandad,
> Thank you for your letter. Yes, I'm fine but I had a terrible shock last night.
> You know that Mrs Richards, my landlady, had a car accident last week and is in hospital now? Well, that means that I have to cook my own dinner, and yesterday evening I burnt it. I decided to buy some fish and chips instead, but when I went to the shop I think I left the front door open. When I came back I saw a light in Mrs Richards' room. I ran upstairs, but it wasn't Mrs Richards. Someone was standing in the room, opening all the drawers, and putting things in <u>my</u> suitcase. Suddenly the stranger turned towards me. I couldn't see the person's face because there was a scarf over the nose and mouth, but I did see something heavy and grey in one hand. I shut the door, turned the key and telephoned the police.
> When they arrived I opened the door. The stranger was under the bed. I listened to the conversation

Listen to what Keith heard.

2 Fill the form

When Keith rang the police station the policeman filled in a form.
Here it is. Can you fill it in? Put a tick (✓) in the correct box.

REPORTED BREAK-IN					
PLACE	TIME	HOW DID THE INTRUDER GET IN?	ANYTHING TAKEN?	REPORTED BY	
Shop ☐	Morning ☐	Broke a window ☐	Clothes ☐	The owner of the property	☐
Hotel ☐	Mid-day ☐	Broke a door ☐	Money ☐	Another person living on the property	☐
House ☐	Afternoon ☐	Broke a lock ☐	Furniture ☐		
Flat ☐	Evening ☐	Through an open window ☐	Food and drink ☐	A person working on the property	☐
School ☐	Late at Night ☐	Roof ☐	Jewellery ☐		
Office ☐		Other (give details) ☐	Other (give details) ☐	A neighbour	☐
Factory ☐				A passer-by	☐
Other ☐				Other (give details)	☐

3 Talk to the police

The policeman rang Keith's landlady at the hospital. What did she say?

Policeman: Are you Mrs Richards?
Mrs Richards: Yes, I am.
Policeman: Will you answer a few questions?
Mrs Richards: Yes, I will.
Policeman: Is there a young man living in your house?
Mrs Richards:
Policeman: What is his name?
Mrs Richards:
Policeman: Have you got a niece?
Mrs Richards:
Policeman: Did you see her today?
Mrs Richards:
Policeman: Where did you see her?
Mrs Richards:
Policeman: Why was she there?
Mrs Richards:
Policeman: Did you ask her to do anything?
Mrs Richards:
Policeman: What did you ask her to do?
Mrs Richards:
Policeman: Why did you want them?
Mrs Richards:
Policeman: What did you give her?
Mrs Richards:
Policeman: Shall I send your things to the hospital?
Mrs Richards:

4 Who said what?

The policeman talked to Keith, Mrs Richards and her niece. He wrote their answers in his notebook. Here are some of the things he wrote. Who said what?

a) It was *my* suitcase.
b) I burnt my dinner.
c) I went under the bed to get the slippers.
d) I tore my dress in the accident.
e) I gave her the key.
f) There was nobody in, and the door was open.
g) I thought it was a gun.
h) The light was on upstairs.
i) There wasn't any money in my purse.
j) I had a tooth out.

5 Sort it out

Keith telephoned his mother, but he was still very upset, and his sentences were all mixed up. What was he trying to say?

a) My landlady is   at the upstairs window.
b) I left my dinner   under the bed.
c) I bought some supper   from the drawers.
d) I saw a light   in her hand.
e) Someone was taking things   in the bedroom.
f) She was putting them   over her face.
g) I thought she had a gun   at the fish and chip shop.
h) She had a scarf   in bed at the hospital.
i) I locked her   in the oven.
j) When the police arrived she was   in my suitcase.

6 What did he take?

Keith took Mrs Richards' things to the hospital. He made a list. Mrs Richards wanted something: to read
to eat
to spend
to tell the time with
to wash her face with
to clean her teeth with
to write with
to wear on her feet
to wear in bed
to wear when she comes home
to carry things in
to do

What did Keith take?

7 Work it out

Keith decided to take some puzzles for Mrs Richards. Here is one of them: Get from *car* to *bed* in three moves. Every move must be an English word.

```
         C A R
   (i)   B A R
   (ii)  B A D
   (iii) B E D
```

Here are four more. Can you do the puzzles?

Get from *home* to *comb* in two moves.
Get from *step* to *shoe* in three moves.
Get from *chip* to *when* in four moves.
Get from *can* to *not* in four moves.

UNIT FIVE
We can use the school hall

1 Listen
There is going to be a fete at Turnham village on Saturday, and Linda and Anne are on the committee. It is going to be quite a big fete with competitions, games and races at the sports centre, and stalls on the playing-field.

Everything is ready. Then on Friday night Linda telephones Anne.

Listen to their conversation.

2 Plan the hall
Here is Anne's plan of the hall from last year. Can you decide where the stalls are going to be on Saturday?

Table 1 *sweets and balloons*
Table 2 *toys*
Table 3 *cakes*
Table 4 *table and chairs*
Table 5 *Groceries*
Table 6 *Groceries*
Table 7 *toys*
Small table 8 *teas*
Small table 9 *plants*
stage : Fortune-telling

3 Tell the stallholders
Here is a list of all the people who are running stalls tomorrow:

Balloons	Mr Peters
Cakes	Mrs Anderson
Toys	Ms Williams
Plants	Mrs Smith
Sweets	Mr Griffiths
Books	Ms Green
Teas	Mrs Waters and Miss O'Neil
Fortune-telling	Miss Trapp
Groceries	Mr Baker and Mrs Brown

Here is what Anne said to three of the people:
—Mr Peters, your stall will be in the same place this year.
—Mrs Anderson, your stall will be near the window this year.
—Ms Williams, your stall will be beside the sweets and balloons this year.

What did she say to the others?

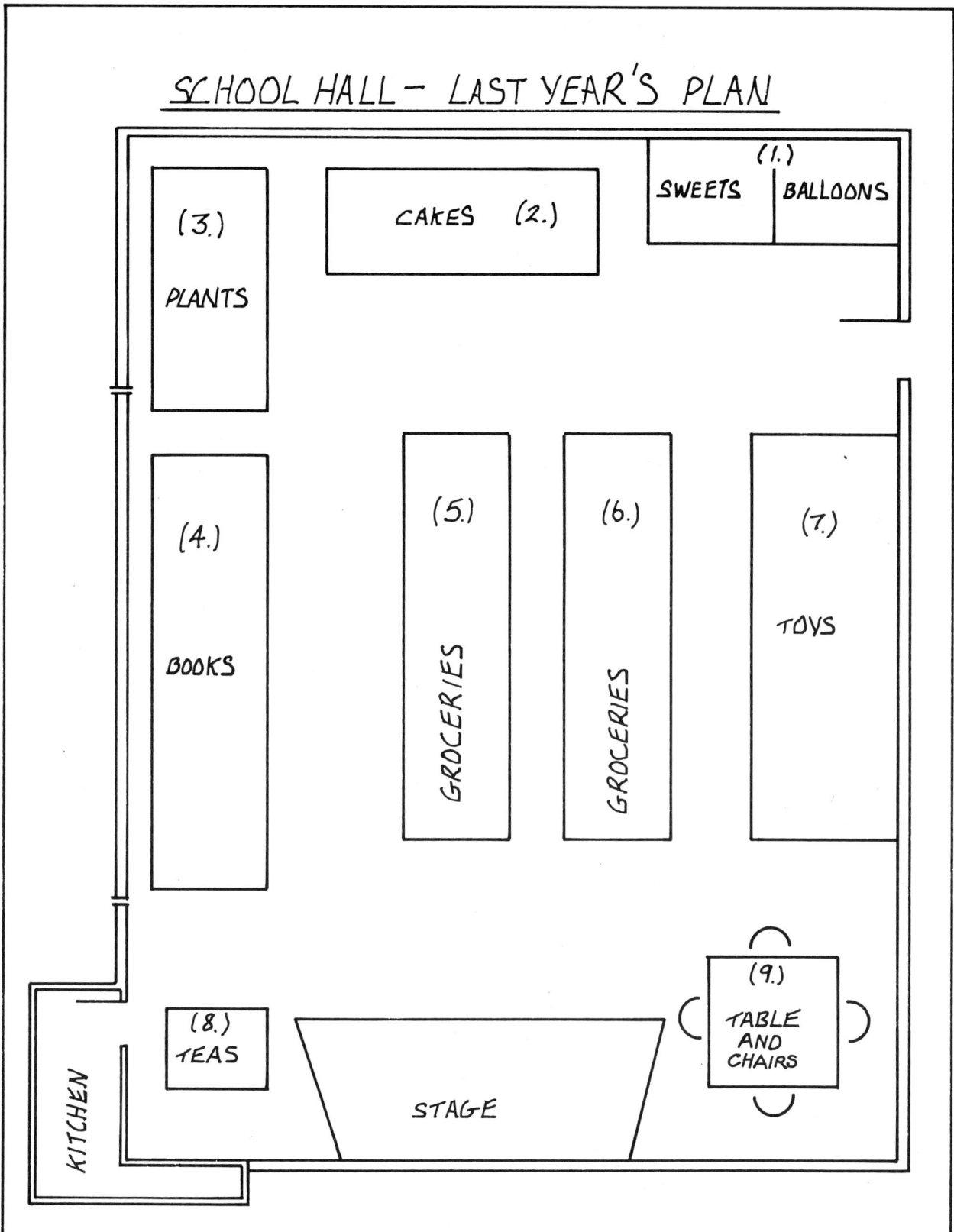

4 Tell their fortunes

Before Anne went to bed she made a fortune-telling card. Here it is:

| You will | meet
marry
be
win
find
buy
lose
eat | a
an | famous
beautiful
strong
wonderful
enormous
big
expensive
handsome | millionaire
film star
prince
princess
diamond
horse
stranger
dinner
watch |

Her fortune-telling stall was very busy. Linda came, and her mother, her young brother, her husband and her ten-year-old son. There were also ten strangers. Can you help Anne tell their fortunes for them?

5 What do they want?

At the fete lots of people asked Linda to buy things for them.

- Linda's mother said,   'I want twelve little ones with icing on them.'
- Her father said,   'I want six healthy ones with red flowers.'
- Her young brother said,   'I want a big blue one with a long string.'
- Her son said,   'I want a famous one with a good story.'
- Linda's sister said,   'I want some that I can cook for supper.'
- Her young daughter said,   'I want one with furry arms and glass eyes.'
- Anne said,   'I want a hot one, with milk and sugar.'

What did she buy for each person?

6 Read the words

At the fete Linda bought a book for her son. But there is a strip missing from one of the pages. Can you help him read it?

> John shut the door and ran quickl
> down the street. He went to the hous
> and took his torch and a strong pie
> of string. Then he ran straight ba
> to the garden.
> The stranger was still there.
> was holding something in his h
> At first John thought it was o
> of his father's strawberries.
> That's strange he th
> But then he looked more caref
> 'It's the diamond!' he said.

7 Competition

Here is one of the competitions from the fete:
'How many English words do you know which begin with the letters STR?'
(six is good, eight is very good, more than eight is excellent)

strange   strong
stranger   strike
street   str
string
straight
strawberries

UNIT SIX
Miles from anywhere

1 Listen

Larry's parents have just bought a new house in Brenton, and Larry is helping them move the furniture. He has hired a van and he has already moved most of the furniture into the new house. Larry's parents are spending the day with a friend who lives quite near the new house. At about midnight, Larry telephones the friend's house and speaks to his mother.

Listen to their conversation.

2 Listen and answer

Larry's mother tried to explain the problem to her friend. But her friend kept asking questions. Answer the questions.

a) Where is he?
b) Where is the nearest petrol station?
c) Why doesn't he go there?
d) Why can't he buy any petrol?
e) Why can't he catch a bus?
f) Do you know where there is any petrol?
g) Why don't you drive his car to the van?
h) Can he get a lift?
i) Does he want a taxi?
j) What is he going to do?

3 Find the answer

Can you find a better solution to Larry's problems?

4 Put them in the right place

In the new house a lot of things are in the hall. Larry did not know where to put them. Can you help him put the things in the right rooms before his mother arrives? Some of them can go in more than one room.

Rooms
Kitchen
Bathroom
Bedroom
Sitting room
Dining room

Things
Toothpaste
Knives
Cushions
Pillows
Saucepans
Radio
Forks
Bookcase
Flour
Shampoo
Slippers
Alarm clock
Tablecloths
Kettle
Television
Towels

5 What have you done with...?

Before Larry and his father went back to the van, Larry's father asked him a lot of questions:
He asked, 'What have you done with the van?'
Larry said, 'I've left it beside the road.'

Here are some more questions his father asked. What do you think Larry said?

a) What have you done with the key of the house?
b) What have you done with the key of the garage?
c) What have you done with the furniture from the old house?
d) What have you done with your wallet?
e) What have you done with your bicycle?
f) What have you done with the can of petrol?
g) What have you done with the key of the van?

6 Sort it out

While Larry and his father went to the van, Larry's mother talked to her friend. Her friend talks all the time. Today she talked about her sister, her cat, and her baby granddaughter. Larry's mother did not know which sentences were about the sister, which sentences were about the cat, and which sentences were about the granddaughter. Can you help?

She has only got three legs.   Sometimes she bites her toes.   She hasn't got any teeth.   She speaks three languages.   She wakes up in the night and screams.   Sometimes she chases mice.   She drives a red sports car.   She has a furry tail.   She has a red face and no hair.   She is fifty years old.   She plays the piano.   I like to see her in the bath.   She has long white whiskers.   Sometimes she climbs trees and walks on the piano.

7 Find the message

When Larry got back to the van, he found a note on it. The note was from a friend of his. This is what it said:

UNIT SEVEN
The monster will come back!

1 Read and listen
Here is an advertisement for a television programme:

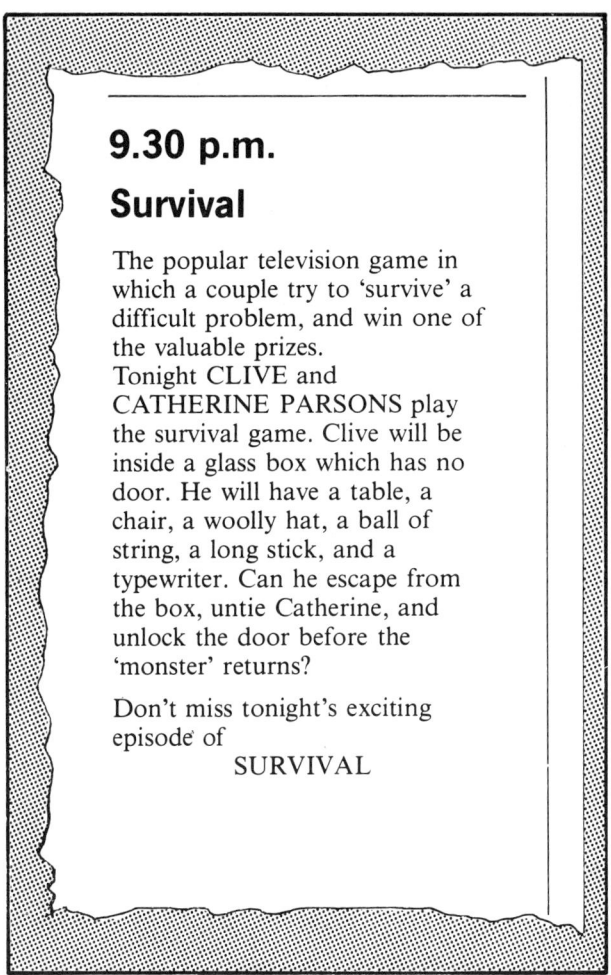

9.30 p.m.

Survival

The popular television game in which a couple try to 'survive' a difficult problem, and win one of the valuable prizes.
Tonight CLIVE and CATHERINE PARSONS play the survival game. Clive will be inside a glass box which has no door. He will have a table, a chair, a woolly hat, a ball of string, a long stick, and a typewriter. Can he escape from the box, untie Catherine, and unlock the door before the 'monster' returns?

Don't miss tonight's exciting episode of
   SURVIVAL

Listen to part of the programme.

2 Listen for the suggestions
Each team loses two points for every incorrect suggestion. Clive and Catherine lose sixteen points. Can you find all their incorrect suggestions?

3 Find the letter

Here is a picture of a typewriter. Do you know which letter Clive has to push? (Look at the typewriter keyboard and think carefully about the words 'push the *right* letter'.)

4 Make suggestions

When Clive has untied Catherine, he has to unlock the door. But the key is in a very deep box full of water. Catherine and Clive can't see into the box because it is too tall. They know the key is in the water, but they can't reach it. Make some suggestions:

–Try ____
–What about ____?
–Why don't you ____?
–You could ____
–Can you ____?
–Perhaps you can ____
–If you ____

(Don't forget the things that were on the table.)

5 Sort it out

At last Clive and Catherine find another piece of paper. On the paper there are some instructions. But they are mixed up. Can you help them find the right instructions before the monster arrives?

a) If you look inside the woollen hat   you will see into the water.
b) If you tie it to the string   the monster will catch you.
c) If you stand on the chair   it will reach the key.
d) If you put the string into the water   you will find a hook.
e) If you are careful   you will make a fishing line.
f) If you pull it out   you will be able to pick up the key.
g) If you take too long   the door will soon be open.

6 Describe the monster

Clive and Catherine take the key and go to the door. But they cannot put the key into the keyhole. In the hole there is a piece of paper. This is what it says:

The monster is *dalb*. He has *igehente* fingers and long *depinot* toes. His teeth are *prash*, but he has no *eons*. He has a *dornu* body, but his legs are *nith*. He has a *glon* tail and *umorneso* eyes. He is very *rygede* and *urcle*. If he is *nurghy* he will eat you.

What does the message say?

7 Work it out

At last Clive and Catherine open the door – just in time. They win one of the prizes. In the square you will find the names of the prizes. You can read up and down, or left to right. All the prizes begin with the letter 'C'. There are fourteen prizes. Can you find ten of them?

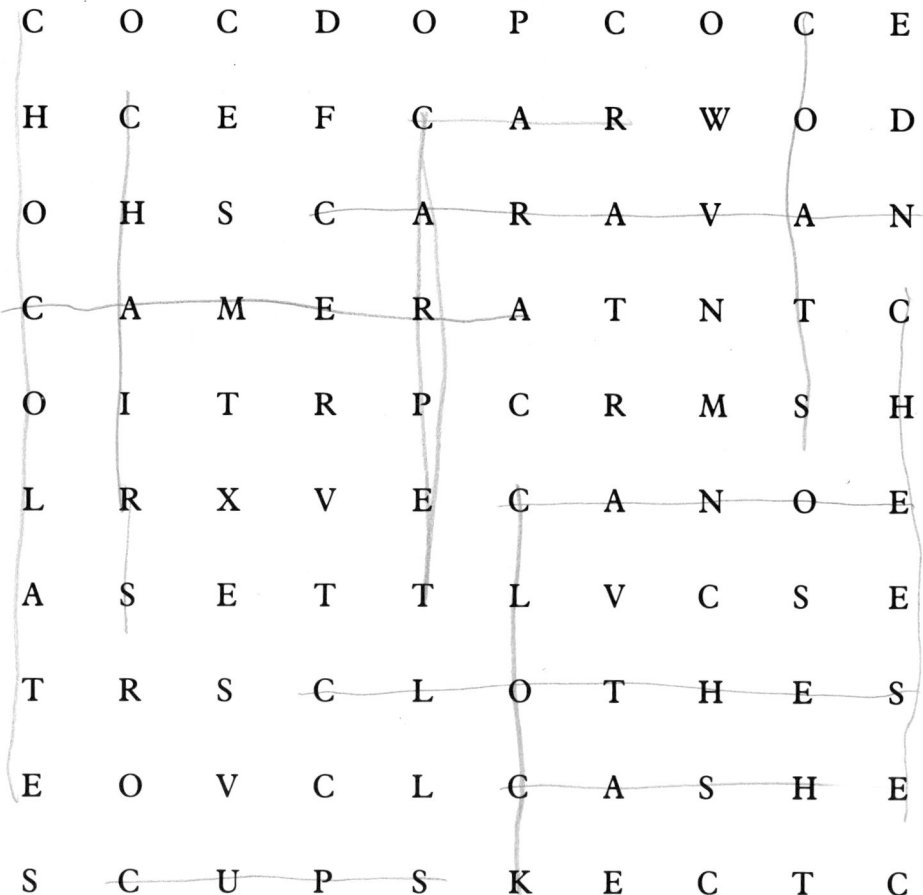

```
C  O  C  D  O  P  C  O  C  E
H  C  E  F  C  A  R  W  O  D
O  H  S  C  A  R  A  V  A  N
C  A  M  E  R  A  T  N  T  C
O  I  T  R  P  C  R  M  S  H
L  R  X  V  E  C  A  N  O  E
A  S  E  T  T  L  V  C  S  E
T  R  S  C  L  O  T  H  E  S
E  O  V  C  L  C  A  S  H  E
S  C  U  P  S  K  E  C  T  C
```

31

UNIT EIGHT
There must be some mistake

1 Listen

Martin Johnson is the manager of an employment agency. People who want a job come to his office, and Martin writes some information about each person on a card. Then he puts the information into the computer. When someone telephones the office and asks for a person to do a job, Martin programs the computer to find the right person for the job.

But this morning it is different. Martin picks up the telephone and this is the conversation…

2 Listen and write

This is Martin's information about J.V. Brown:

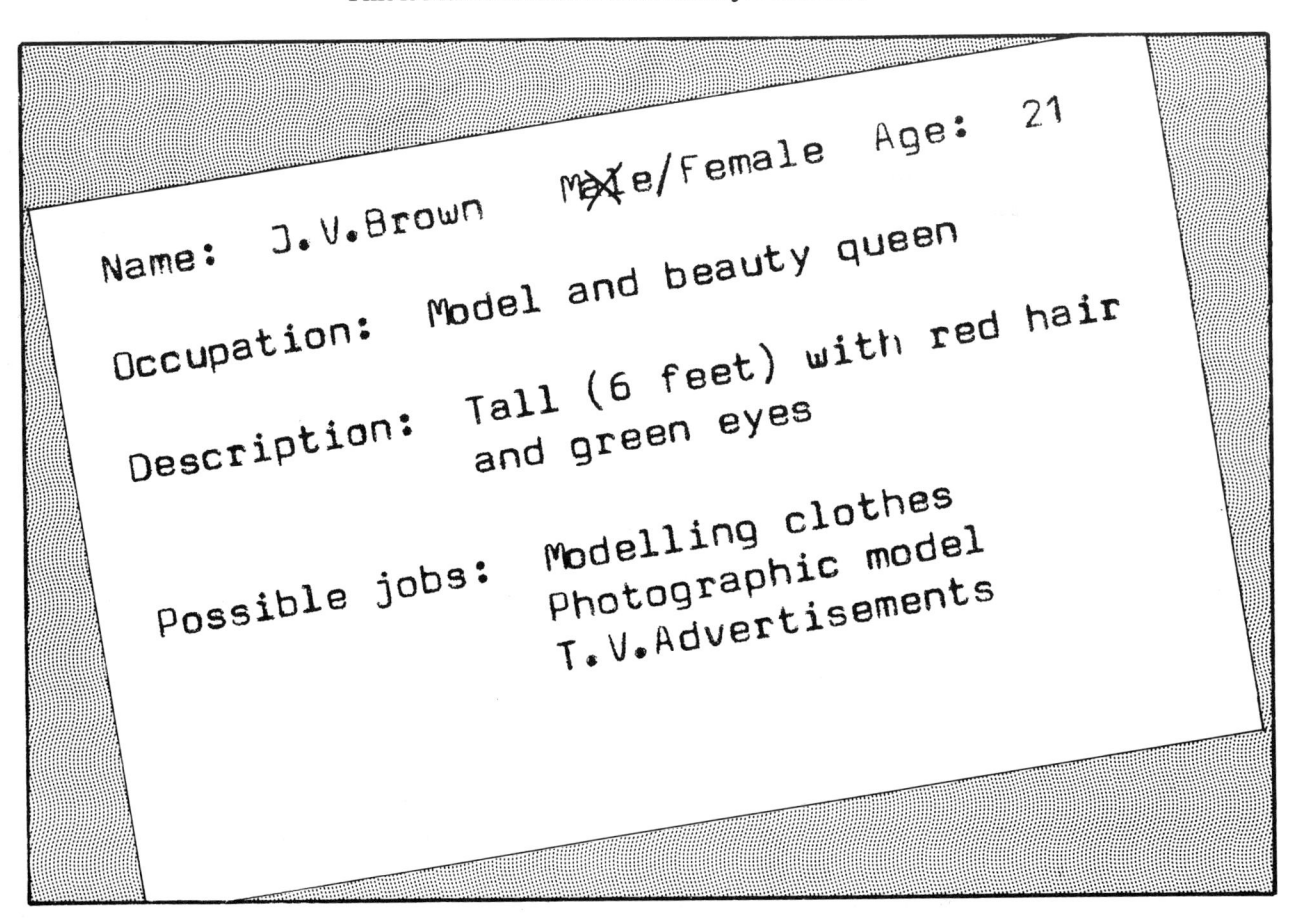

Name: J.V.Brown   Male/Female   Age: 21
Occupation: Model and beauty queen
Description: Tall (6 feet) with red hair and green eyes
Possible jobs: Modelling clothes
Photographic model
T.V. Advertisements

Now complete this card for J.V. Brown:

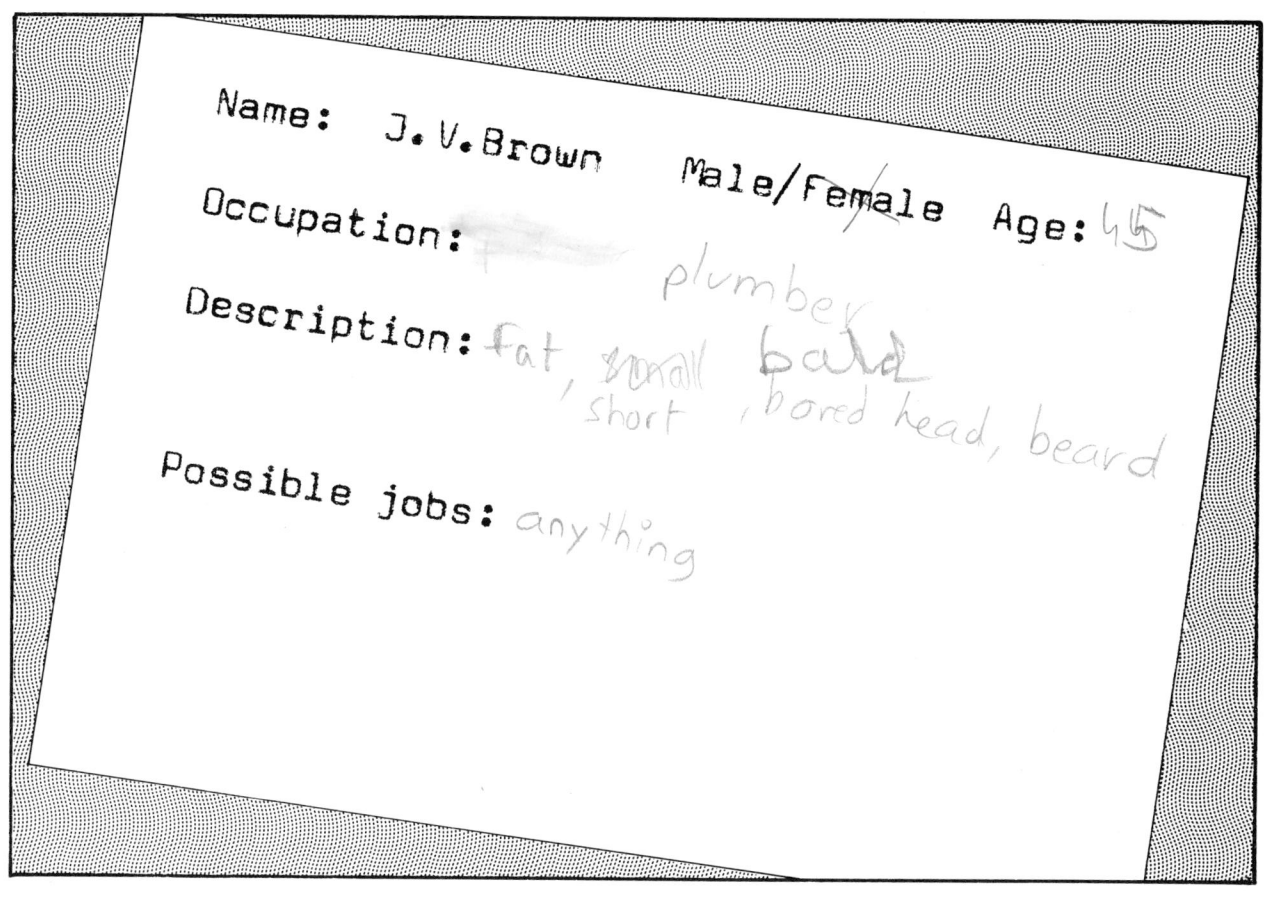

3 Who said what?

That evening Martin, the plumber and the photographer all talked about their interesting morning. Here is what they said. Who said what?

a) I put on the dress and the necklace and waited.
b) When I saw him, I started to laugh.
c) I took a photograph of him anyway.
d) I had two cards about J.V. Brown.
e) The dress was too tight for me.
f) I left a note when I went to get the film.
g) The photographer telephoned me.
h) I thought it was an advertisement for something.
i) I sent the wrong person.

4 Ask the questions

Martin first spoke to the beauty queen on the telephone. She gave him the information on the computer card. First he asked, 'What's your name?' What other questions did he ask?

5 Sort it out

Martin has a list of people and a list of jobs. Has he got the right people to do all the jobs? Help him sort out his list.

He has
- a gardener 4
- a plumber 7
- a carpenter 6
- an electrician 1
- a mechanic 2
- an architect 8
- a cook 3
- a clown 9
- a nurse 5

- to mend the lights 1
- to change a wheel 2
- to roast a chicken 3
- to plant some trees 4
- to bath an old lady 5
- to fall into the custard 6
- to mend the bath 7
- to plan a building 8
- to play the violin 9

What has he got wrong?

6 What do they do?

Martin is very careful. He looks at the people before they go to their jobs. This is what he sees. Who are they?

A, who is young and dark-haired and is carrying a hammer.
B, who is very short and fat, has a red nose and big feet.
C, who is middle-aged with a kind face and is wearing a white apron.
D, who is big and strong, is carrying a spade.
E, who is small and bearded, is carrying a bag of spanners and taps.
F, who is young and good-looking, is carrying a big drawing-board.
G, who is elderly and plump, is carrying a screwdriver and some wire.
H, who is tall and good-looking, is wearing a dirty overall and carrying a spanner.
I, who is tiny and thin, is wearing a white overall, and carrying a recipe book.

7 Work it out

Martin sometimes wants to write things which are not very polite. He has a secret code. Can you understand it?

a) Someone who is not thin is

b) Someone who has no hair is

c) Someone who is not good is

d) Someone who is not pretty is

e) Someone who is not tall is

f) Someone who doesn't want to work is

g) Someone who is not young is

h) Someone who is not sensible is

Write down the letters which the symbols represent.

UNIT NINE
The ugliest jug you've ever seen!

1 Listen

Sarah is the manager of a successful business in a small town in the south of England. She collects beautiful jugs. She has nearly two hundred of them, and some are very valuable.

Her friend, Elizabeth, has an antique shop in a nearby town. She often telephones Sarah and tells her about interesting jugs which come into her shop. But one day Sarah telephones Elizabeth.

Listen to their conversation.

2 Listen and answer

Later, Sarah telephoned her boyfriend, Justin, and told him about the jug. But it was a bad telephone line and he couldn't hear her very well. He asked a lot of questions. What did Sarah say?

Justin: Who is coming to stay with you?
Sarah:

Justin: Why?
Sarah:

Justin: Didn't she give you a jug before?
Sarah:

Justin: What did you do with it?
Sarah:

Justin: Why?
Sarah:

Justin: Who bought it?
Sarah:

Justin: Why?
Sarah:

Justin: How much did he pay?
Sarah:

Justin: Where is it now?
Sarah:

Justin: Why?
Sarah:

Justin: What is she going to do with it?
Sarah:

3 Fill the form

Sarah went to the market. She wanted a jug *exactly* like the other one. The lady at the market gave her a form. Can you help her complete it?

What kind of object do you want?	
What do you expect the price to be?	Minimum: Maximum:
Any particular colour?	
Pattern?	
Any unusual features?	

Why do you think Sarah tried to buy another jug?

4 Think about it!
- How much money did the man in Plymouth make?
- How much did Elizabeth make?
- How much has Aunt Mary paid for the jug?   (Think carefully!)

5 Tell the story
Three weeks later Elizabeth telephoned Sarah. She asked about Aunt Mary. Sarah told her the whole story but the sentences here are in the wrong order. What happened?

- I said that she had a kind heart.
- She asked me where the other one was.
- She said that she knew a shop in Plymouth which sold them.
- I told her that it was broken.
- She said that there was a jug inside it.
- She asked if I would carry her suitcase.
- She told me that there was a pig on the handle.
- She told me not to drop it.
- She said that it was for me.
- She said that it had an ugly face.
- She said that it was exactly like the one I had.
- She told me that she would buy me another one.

6 What did they say?
Elizabeth found the telephone number of the antique shop in Plymouth. She rang the owner.

Elizabeth: Are you the man who came to my shop last week?

Owner: Yes, I am.

Elizabeth: Do you remember the ugly jug with the pig on the handle?

Owner: Yes, I do.

Elizabeth: Have you still got it?

Owner: No, I haven't.

Elizabeth: Where is it?

Owner: Mary Withers, one of my customers, has it. She is looking for more china with the same pattern.

Elizabeth told Sarah about the conversation. She began:
'I asked if he was the man who came to my shop. He said that he was.'
What else did she say?

7 Work it out

Two weeks later Sarah received a letter from her Aunt Mary. But Aunt Mary is not a good typist. She always types 'J', 'K' and 'S' instead of three of the vowels. Find out which vowels are typed incorrectly. What does the letter say?

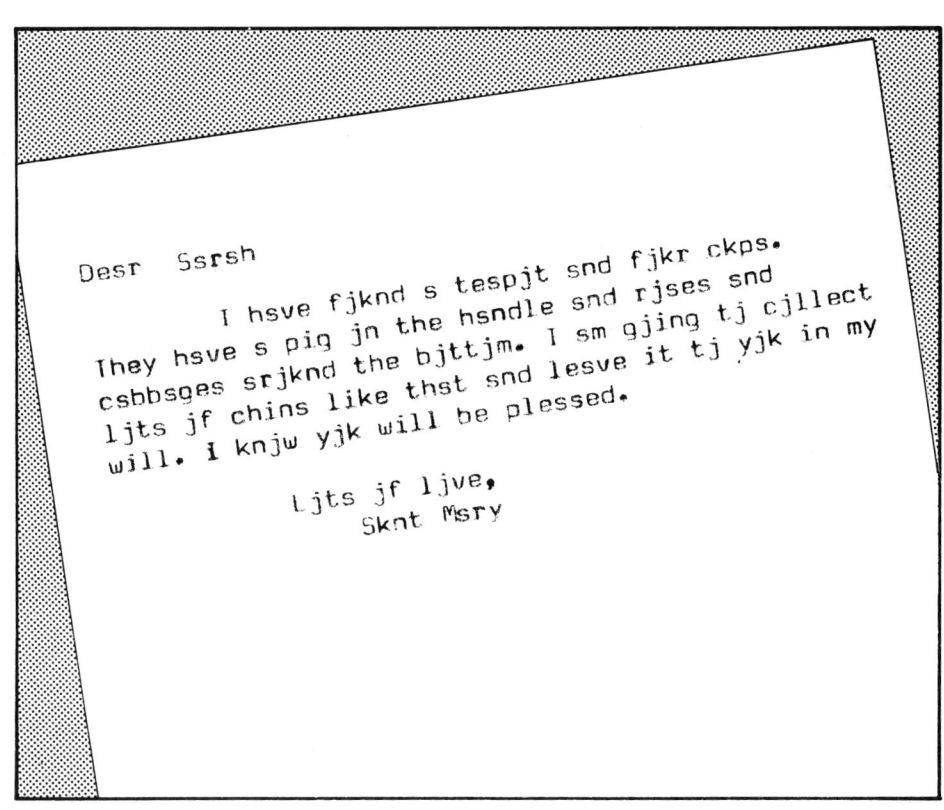

Desr Ssrsh

I hsve fjknd s tespjt snd fjkr ckps. They hsve s pig jn the hsndle snd rjses snd csbbsges srjknd the bjttjm. I sm gjing tj cjllect ljts jf chins like thst snd lesve it tj yjk in my will. I knjw yjk will be plessed.

Ljts jf ljve,
Sknt Msry

UNIT TEN
Amazing Journey

1 Listen

Stephen Taylor is a famous canoeist. He has just returned to England after an amazing journey in his canoe. He went with some friends to one of the highest mountains in Africa, and three of them came down the mountainside by canoe, on one of the rivers. The journey down the mountain took five days. The canoeists took a camera with them and made a film of their amazing trip. When Stephen arrived at London Airport after the adventure, a radio reporter was waiting for him.

Look at your map and listen to their conversation.

2 Follow the route

The reporter has this map of Stephen's journey. It shows the path which the walkers took. He wants to print it in his newspaper, but he wants to add some information. Can you help him mark these things on his map?

A —This is where the aeroplane landed.

B —This is where one canoeist lost his canoe.

C —There is ice in the water here.

D —This is where one walker broke his leg.

E —There is some beautiful scenery here.

F —The water is very fast-moving here.

G —Day One   (write ⟵⟶)

H —Day Two

I —End of Day Three

J —Days Four and Five

3 Who is missing?

A photographer took pictures of the travellers before and after the trip. When they began their journey there were two groups of travellers.

Group 1 (Canoeists) **Group 2 (Walkers)**
S. Taylor W. Williams
P. Smith K. Peters
J. Johnson M. Phillips

When they arrived, the two groups were different. Can you help the photographer finish this list?

Group 1 **Group 2**
S. Taylor W. Williams
J. Johnson K. Peters

4 This is my life!

A young man heard the report and wanted to join Stephen's next canoe journey. The young man made some notes on a piece of paper about his experience as a canoeist. This is what he wrote:

Then he wrote a letter:

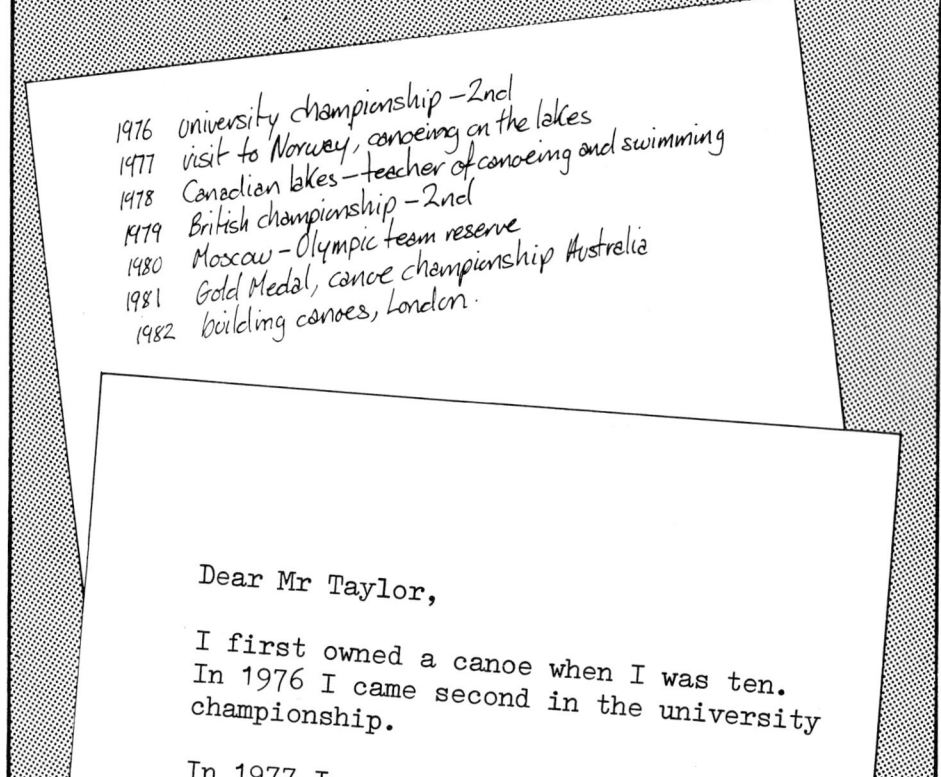

Can you help him finish his letter?

5 Sort it out

Stephen asked the young man, 'If you come on this journey, what will you need?' The young man gave a good list, but he was nervous and he gave the wrong reasons. Can you help him?

a) a woollen hat   to ride in
b) a strong canoe   to cook the food
c) a lightweight tent   to wear
d) a good paddle   to eat
e) a waterproof suit   for the canoe
f) a pair of gloves   to sleep in
g) a portable camping stove   to keep your hands warm
h) plenty of food   to put on your head

6 Answer the questions

The young man's mother is not very happy. She is sure that there will be an accident. She asks a lot of questions. What do you think the young man says? (Try to start your answers with 'if'.)

–Will you go if Mr Taylor asks you?
–Where will you sleep if it rains?
–What will you do if it snows?
–What will you do if you fall into the river?
–What will happen if you meet a wild animal?
–What will you do if you lose your paddle?
–How will I know if you have an accident?
–What will happen if you damage your canoe?
–What will happen if you break your leg?
–How can you use a camera if you are paddling a canoe?

7 Find the message

Stephen sent a telex to the young man. But someone made a mistake. What did the telex say, and what was the mistake?

```
R O L Y A T N E H P E T S S R U O Y

T S I E O N A C R E H T O N A D E E N E W

E C N O T A E M O C E S A E L P S E Y
```

UNIT ELEVEN
Consolidation: Anyone for cricket?

1 Listen
Timothy Grey is a teacher. He loves cricket. He plays every Saturday afternoon at the cricket club in the town. He is a good batsman, but he is not in the team because there are other people who are better than he is.

One Saturday morning the captain telephones Timothy.

Listen to their conversation.

2 What does Timothy need?
Timothy sits down to make a list of all the things he needs, and where they are. There are ten things he needs. Can you help him list them? Where are they?

3 Help Timothy
Look at the map. Which is the quickest route for Timothy to take?

4 Sort it out
Timothy does not have an easy day. Everywhere he goes he finds a problem. Can you match the items to the problems?

a) The garage mechanics   hurt his feet.
b) His shirt   is full of rubbish.
c) His trousers   have gone out.
d) His mother and father   have got holes in the legs.
e) His bag   is full of people.
f) The post office   is playing cricket.
g) His cap   is covered in wet paint.
h) His brother   is locked up in the school.
i) The pavilion   hasn't got any buttons.
j) His shoes   have lost the car keys.

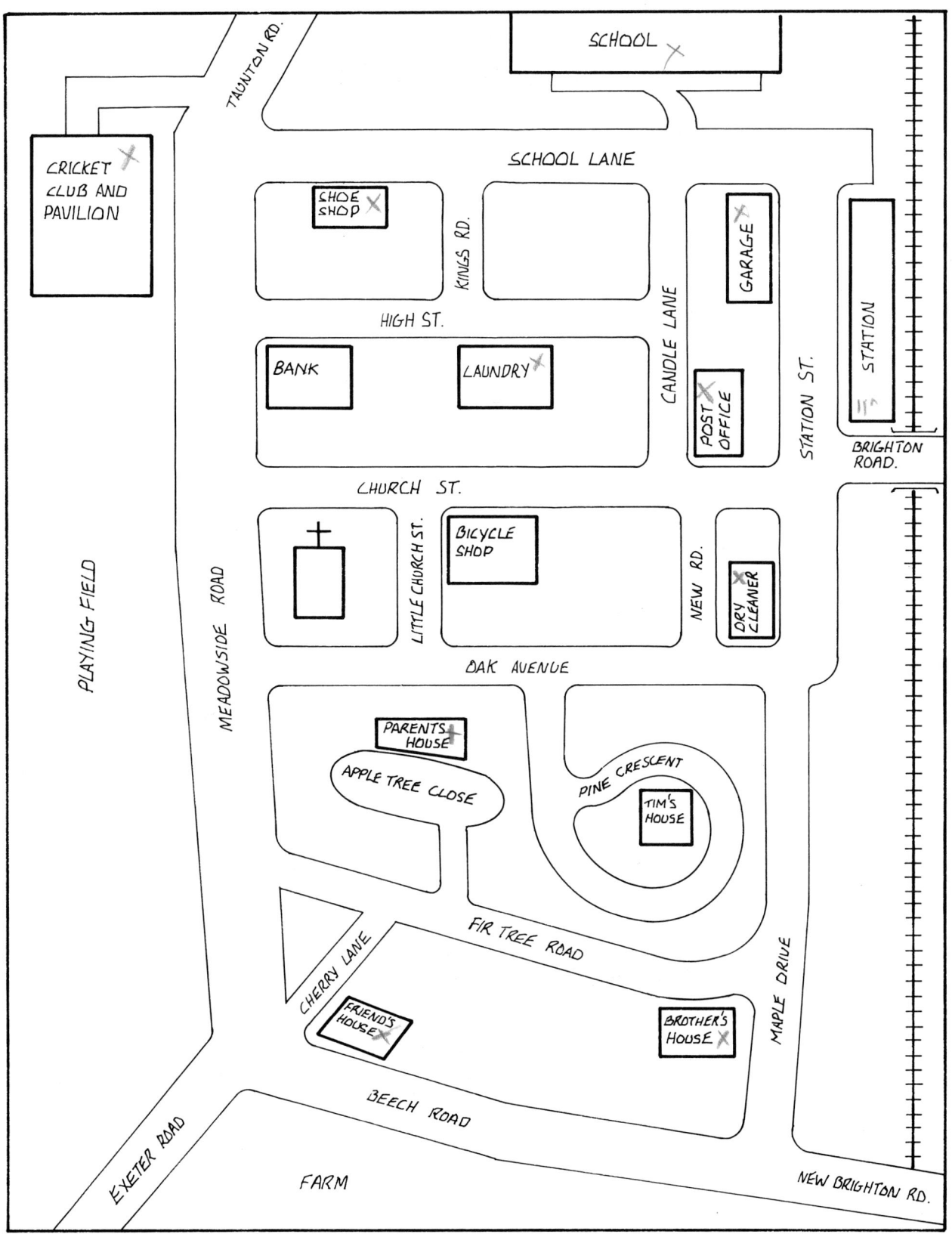

5 What's wrong now?

Timothy borrows everything from his brother, takes his bat and catches the train. But his troubles have not finished. He finds that:

—the cap is too small
—the pullover is too wide
—the collar is too tight
—the sleeves are too long
—the trousers are too loose
—the legs are too short
—the shoes are too big

Timothy explains that these clothes belong to his brother. 'You don't know him', he says. 'I know a lot about your brother,' says the captain. 'His head is smaller than yours.' What else does the captain know?

6 Talk to the press

Timothy plays very well, and scores a lot of runs. Everyone is very pleased, especially Timothy. A journalist interviews him after the game. What does Timothy say?

Journalist: Are you Timothy Grey?
Timothy: Yes, I am.
Journalist: And you scored 100 runs this afternoon?
Timothy: Yes, I did.
Journalist: Did you expect to score 100?
Timothy:
Journalist: Have you ever scored 100 runs before?
Timothy:
Journalist: Do you always play in the team?
Timothy:
Journalist: Have you ever played in the team before?
Timothy:
Journalist: Would you like to play in the team again?
Timothy:
Journalist: Do you think you'll be in the team again?
Timothy:
Journalist: Are you pleased with this afternoon's game?
Timothy:
Journalist: Do you usually wear a small cap and an enormous pullover?
Timothy:
Journalist: Why are you wearing them today?
Timothy:

7 What can you see?

On the way home they looked out of the train window. This is a picture of what they saw. Simon said, 'I can see a batsman and bowler.'

How many things can you see which begin with 'b'? (There are more than twenty.)